OTABIND

Dear Friend:

You may have noticed th[...] [...] than most other quality paperba[...] [...]tance, along with the back page, is [...] [...] en the book the spine "floats" in back of the pages. But there's nothing wrong with your book. These features allow us to produce what is known as a detached cover, specifically designed to prevent the spine from cracking even after repeated use. A state-of-the-art binding technology known as OtaBind® is used in the manufacturing of this and all Health Communications, Inc. books.

HCI has invested in equipment and resources that ensure the books we produce are of the highest quality, yet remain affordable. At our Deerfield Beach headquarters, our editorial and art departments are just a few steps from our pressroom, bindery and shipping facilities. This internal production enables us to pay special attention to the needs of our readers when we create our books.

Our titles are written to help you improve the quality of your life. You may find yourself referring to this book repeatedly, and you may want to share it with family and friends who can also benefit from the information it contains. For these reasons, our books have to be durable and, more importantly, user-friendly.

OtaBind® gives us these qualities. Along with a crease-free spine, the book you have in your hands has some other characteristics you may not be aware of:

- Open the book to any page and it will lie flat, so you'll never have to worry about losing your place.
- You can bend the book over backwards without damage, allowing you to hold it with one hand.
- The spine is 3-5 times stronger than conventional perfect binding, preventing damage even with rough handling.

This all adds up to a better product for our readers—one that will last for years to come. We stand behind the quality of our books and guarantee that, if you're not completely satisfied, we'll replace the book or refund your money within 30 days of purchase. If you have any questions about this guarantee or our bookbinding process, please feel free to contact our customer service department at 1-800-851-9100.

We hope you enjoy the quality of this book, and find understanding, insight and direction for your life in the information it provides.

Health Communications, Inc.®

3201 S.W. 15th Street
Deerfield Beach, FL 33442-8190
(305) 360-0909

Peter Vegso
President

MAKE AN APPOINTMENT
WITH YOURSELF

You make an appointment with your dentist . . .
You make an appointment with your mechanic . . .

MAKE AN APPOINTMENT WITH YOURSELF

Simple Steps To Positive Self-Esteem

Maida Berenblatt
Alena Joy Berenblatt

Health Communications, Inc.®
Deerfield Beach, Florida

Library of Congress Cataloging-in-Publication Data

Berenblatt, Maida
        Make an appointment with yourself: simple steps to positive
self-esteem/Maida Berenblatt, Alena Joy Berenblatt.
                p. cm.
        ISBN 1-55874-319-7: $7.95
        1. Self-esteem. I. Berenblatt, Alena Joy.II. Title.
BF697.5S46B47 1994
158'.1--dc20   94-31966
                                                                CIP

© 1994 Maida Berenblatt and Alena Joy Berenblatt
ISBN 1-55874-319-7

Publisher: Health Communications, Inc.
        3201 S.W. 15th Street
        Deerfield Beach, Florida 33442-8190

Cover design by Andrea Perrine Brower

MAKE AN APPOINTMENT WITH YOURSELF

TABLE OF CONTENTS

INTRODUCTION

If this book interests you, it must be time for you to take a long look inward at the way you feel about yourself. You are the source of your self-esteem; only you have the power to feel good about who you are. We hope this book will help in that process. The following story demonstrates a common theme among people with low self-esteem: There is a cause and effect relationship between a child's performance level and parental expectations.

His parents called him Junior and had high hopes he would be someone special. He was the center of his family's attention for five years, until he went to school where no one called him Junior.

Eager to fulfill everyone's expectations, Junior tried to be the best both in the classroom and on the playing field. Often his reach exceeded his abilities, resulting in a series of failures and disappointments.

Whenever he did succeed, he thought the achievement was not related to his effort or behavior. "Just luck," he said and shrugged his shoulders. "It does not really count. Besides, if I get too excited, it'll ruin everything."

Over time, his attitude changed. His behavior seemed to shout: "Don't bother even trying. You won't make it!" All of Junior's unexpressed anger, frustrations and feelings of inadequacy began to pile up and build a negative self-image. This inadequate self-image grew and fed his low self-esteem.

Soon, a hard shell began to cover Junior's soft center. His vulnerabilities, insecurities and anger were hidden from all eyes, including his own. The center whispered, "I'm not good enough," and remained hidden and unexamined. The cover hardened further with defensive behaviors and layers of time.

At that point in Junior's life, a time when he was most vulnerable, he was unable to attain his full emotional potential.

Now Junior is a professionally successful adult, yet his self-esteem remains low—negative and untouched.

This story is common. If you can relate to it, we're glad you picked up this book. Tell yourself you are now ready and willing to invest time and energy toward feeling better about yourself. You have the power to work toward change, to examine the origins of your self-image and to enhance the value of your self-esteem.

The self-image you have now is one that you created,

however long ago. Just as you created that one, you can also decide to re-evaluate this self with a current assessment based on adult standards. The approval you seek needs to be redirected away from others toward yourself.

Use this book as a guide. Carry it with you every day. Discover a way to say, "Yes, indeed, I am good enough!" Find a way to love yourself as you wish others to love you. Determine how you can respect and acknowledge your value. Feel good about yourself . . . today.

Chapter 1

SELF AS VALUE

✓ *The quiet integrity*

of self-approval

is more important

than the applause

of many.

Make a mental list of the significant people in your life. Are you on this list? If so, where have you placed yourself? If not, where would you have placed yourself?

Everyone secretly longs to be number one on the list of important people, but they want others to put them there. It's not selfish to make yourself number one. It's an indication of positive self-esteem. Making an appointment with yourself is the first step to being number one. This does not exclude the importance of other people in your life. Instead, it enhances your sense of self and avoids looking to others for your value.

Self-esteem begins in childhood. Children look into their parents' faces for love, assurance and approval. When Mommy or Daddy smiles, a child feels happy. Soon, more people are introduced to the child's world—teachers, baby-sitters, friends—adding even more faces to look to for approval.

During the developing preteen years, children begin to consider how they feel about their relationships with their families. At this point in time, parental statements and behavior play a powerful role in this initial attempt toward positive self-esteem.

Children believe what adults say. They don't have the ability to discriminate facts from opinions. If Mommy is mad at Daddy and tells her child to leave the room, the child thinks, "I am bad." This thought is internalized as a fact and becomes a part of the child's self-image. Equally damaging are feelings of being ignored or having controlling parents who give positive reinforcement only when the child follows rigid standards of behavior.

If these issues—and the negative self-esteem resulting from them—are not resolved in childhood, the memories will continue producing negative self-esteem, even in adulthood. Poor self-esteem is believed to be one reason for failure in school, low occupational aspirations, a willingness to use and abuse alcohol and drugs, and many violent behaviors.

Studies show that even with the finest curriculum development in schools and the best support services in community agencies, it is difficult to shape a young person's direction and motivation for productivity and happiness unless that child has a foundation of positive self-esteem.

Chapter 2

SELF AND ESTEEM

✓ *Your image of you*

comes from within.

It is always a

challenge to listen

to the message.

Your physical appearance, the way you look in the mirror, is the way others see you. Rightly or wrongly, people use your physical appearance to assess your worth as an individual. You are judged by your style of clothes, hair, makeup and body size. For some, this judgment is critical and they may endlessly seek approval from others.

Self-esteem is the way you see yourself, the impression you have of yourself and the expectations you have for yourself. If you believe that you are worthwhile and valuable, approval comes from within, rather than from the opinions and evaluations of others.

Positive self-esteem is accepting yourself and understanding who you are. If you cannot feel good about yourself, it is hard to feel good about your experiences.

Too often, self-esteem is negative because the critical voices from the past are used as guidelines for current self-evaluations. New positive thoughts must replace older negative ones, allowing you to overcome messages from the past affecting today's decisions.

For example, many adults respond in a childlike manner when confronted with a person of authority. When some parents get called to the principal's office, they forget the topic is their child. The parent thinks, "I am not good because my child is not good." And because the parents give the principal authoritative power, they relinquish their own power and communicate less effectively.

Developing positive self-esteem is a process. Please understand this is not a 28-day cure. Your present sense of self is as old as you are. Just as you learned to adopt this picture of yourself, you can learn to adopt another more positive view. You can learn to trust yourself. You are trustworthy.

Take this book with you as your companion in your briefcase or pocketbook. By making an appointment with yourself and committing yourself to creating better self-esteem, you should see gradual changes unfold as your motivation and energy become more spirited.

Chapter 3

TIMELESS SELF

 *Yesterday's experiences are stepping stones for all your tomorrows.*

Two perspectives create your self-esteem: your history and your view of this history. Your history is how you grew up, where and with whom. This history colors your thought patterns, feelings, attitudes and belief systems.

People often rate themselves compared to others: siblings, classmates, friends and neighbors. If as a child you felt inferior, inadequate or simply not good enough—and you gave yourself a bad rating—it affected your performance, self-image and everything you did. If you held onto that childhood bad rating, it still affects everything you do and every relationship you have, even today.

A bad rating is like wearing sunglasses every day. Unlike rose-tinted lenses where everything looks rosy and seems positive, this is a darker negative view that inhibits your self-image, behavior and relationships.

Valerie looks back on her childhood with sadness and pain. Her childhood impression of herself remains the same today. As she did then, she believes now that she's not lovable, valuable or smart.

"I had the need to go to my mother, just lay my head in her lap and feel protected. Something always held me back. I always felt so alone. I just wanted her to love me. I wanted to know I was loved no matter who I was."

Valerie's mother was very critical of everything her daughter did. Valerie believed nothing she did was good enough. Valerie was also criticized in front of her friends, so in addition to feeling inadequate, Valerie felt humiliated.

Their relationship lacked affection. Valerie believed her mother never liked her. And Valerie didn't think her mother was bad. Valerie thought her mother's responses to her were based on her own behavior. Valerie believed that when something wrong happened to her, it was because she didn't do something right.

Valerie's point-of-view and understanding did not tell the whole story.

Actually, Valerie's mother was an alcoholic with little time and energy for her daughter. Her negative behavior and criticisms had little to do with Valerie's behavior, but more to do with her own problems.

Yet throughout Valerie's growing years, her feelings about herself were colored by the childhood perception that she was responsible for everything that happened to her.

Valerie's experience is an example of how self-esteem

can be stripped away over time because of unexamined childhood impressions.

Your first impression of the world often stays with you for many years. If you are the eldest child, you probably felt responsible for younger siblings. That responsibility gave you a sense of competency and efficiency at an early age. The more competent you were, the more people counted on you to do a good job and, consequently, the more jobs you were given. Receiving positive feedback motivated you to maintain your place in the scheme of things.

Eldest children learn to feel good about themselves by taking care of others. Professional positions with heavy responsibilities such as teachers, managers, department heads and CEOs are often held by first-borns.

If a large age gap exists between the first-born and younger children, second-born children can often take on the rewards—and the responsibilities—usually given to the eldest.

If you grew up in poverty and attained wealth later, you may feel different. You may sense something is missing and spend your life trying to find this unattainable something. The feeling of not having enough may always remain.

Adults who were poor children need to assess their life today. Unless they let go of the negative memories of poverty, no amount of money will ever be enough to compensate.

If you are taught to repress your feelings, after a while, you lose touch with them, and you could then become emotionally frozen. Internalized feelings don't go away. They just resurface in many disguises including apathy, depression, psychosomatic illness, anxiety and unhealthy relationships. The repressed child must therefore learn how to express feelings, even though it may be risky, because there is no other way to develop a positive self-esteem.

No single event or person can shape your self-esteem. Your view of your history determines the way you see yourself. If you have not looked at these collected experiences recently, you have the same impression of yourself that you did in childhood. It's time to look again, now. Complete the worksheet that follows.

About You

The purpose of this worksheet is to help you start changing your self-image. Changing the way you think about yourself will help you change the way you behave. Look at your experiences to learn about yourself.

1. Paula was the middle of five children. She learned to watch the behavior of her older sisters as well as her younger brothers. She learned timing, to be insightful and to be intuitive.

What skills did you learn from your birth order position in the family?

2. Steven was everyone's friend. Teachers and classmates alike counted on him to provide a lighter point of view. While he was not a good student, he developed a high level of social skills.

What non-academic skills did you learn in school?

_____

_____

_____

_____

3. Jane is creative with ideas and concepts. David knows how to motivate people and sell, sell, sell. Fran has a pair of hands that can fix anything.

How are you creative?

_____

_____

_____

_____

4. Not all people receive information in the same way. Some need to read it, some need to hear it, some need to sense it and some need to feel it.

How do you best receive information?

_____

_____

_____

_____

5. You may have several views of yourself. If these views are not compatible, they can cause conflict for you. Examine and explore these different views. If they are in harmony, you may reduce your inner conflict.

What is your fantasy of yourself?

How do you think and feel about yourself?

What is the self you present to others?

How do others see you?

6. Maintaining harmony between the views of yourself will be the foundation upon which you can build a healthy opinion of yourself.

What makes you a good friend?

....

....

....

7. What makes you a good employee?

....

....

....

8. Gail is often impatient but is working on improving her patience.
What is difficult for you?

....

....

....

9. Write a brief paragraph about the uniqueness of you. (For example: I am a valuable, lovable, worthwhile person. I deserve to be happy and comfortable.)

....

....

....

....

....

....

....

....

....

Use your own self-assessment as a positive affirmation on the days you feel badly about yourself.

Chapter 4

SELF AS AN AGENT OF CHANGE

True change comes from pain or discomfort.

Everyone agrees that self-esteem is a good thing to have, but it is not clear how to develop it. While developing self-esteem is a process, it starts with these five steps:

Step 1: Identify your needs

Step 2: Fulfill your needs

Step 3: Acknowledge what you did

Step 4: Approve of what you did

Step 5: Share experiences with a friend

Let's take a closer look at each step.

Step One:
Identify Your Needs

Determine what areas in your life you'd like to change. Look at your job, your relationships at home and with friends, the ways in which you manage your day and your feelings and attitudes. If you already know what you need, skip to Step Two.

If you don't know what you want to change, you'll need to continually observe your feelings until you see a pattern of negativity.

Take a notebook and keep it with you for the next seven days. Every day ask yourself, "How would I like my life to be? Using my imagination, what would I like to be doing to feel good about myself?" Jot down the answers and turn the page. Do this every day.

At the end of seven days, open the notebook and review what you have written. You should be able to see a pattern of things you want. Look for a theme. For example, if you have written, "I feel good when I get everything done," this may be a result of the childhood promise, "You can go out to play/have a cookie/watch television when you've finished your chores/homework."

With this focus and your motivation to feel good about yourself, it is possible to identify an unmet need in an area of your life that doesn't work for you. Focusing on your inner self is the first step. Identify one area, one situation, one relationship and the associated feelings.

Step Two:
Fulfill Your Needs

Now that you have identified your needs, it's time to meet them.

Imagine wearing a shoe that doesn't fit. The discomfort makes you feel irritable, annoyed, out of balance or unable to cope. Over time, the ill-fitting shoe may change the shape of your foot, eventually requiring surgical correction.

In this case, the answer seems obvious . . . buy new shoes and throw the old ones away. By translating this example to negative feelings and poor self-esteem, you can see an area in your life needing change. Carrying negative feelings with you each day is unnecessary. Throw those feelings away.

In another example, perhaps you commute to and from work and, after a long day, want a loving greeting when you retun home. Usually you are met at the door with requests, demands or complaints before you even take off your coat. Or, even worse, sometimes there is no acknowledgment you have returned home.

What you would appreciate is a warm greeting, a hug, a smile or some show of affection that helps you join the family with renewed spirit. You have to ask for this. You may have to ask for this more than once, but you have the power to get it.

Once you have identified your needs, fulfill them.

Step Three:
Acknowledge What You Did

Self-acknowledgment is critical to this process of change. It is important to review the steps you took, where they worked for you and where you need improvement. You may realize your fear of change was greater than the actual process of change. Note you were able to move past the fear.

Mark the day of change on your calender. Appreciate your own effort; give yourself a big hug. If others were involved, express appreciation for their participation.

Step Four:
Approve Of What You Did

Moving away from approval-seeking from others toward self-approval is a significant step toward gaining a healthy self-esteem. Because you have set your own guidelines and standards for change, only you should evaluate your performance.

Remember that each time you seek approval from an outside source, you move away from self-validation. Have the courage to trust what you think, see and feel. The integrity of self-approval has greater and more lasting rewards than applause from outside sources.

Now you can experience the exhilarating feeling of knowing you have the power to change. If you can change in one area, you can probably change in others as well.

Step Five:
Share Your Experience With A Friend

This last step may be the most difficult because we have all been taught that bragging or blowing your own horn is conceited or vain. But sharing your accomplishment with a supportive friend creates a positive self-image. And doing it every time you achieve change builds positive self-esteem.

Sharing your experience with a friend may go something like this: "I have learned to do something new, and I would like to share this with you. I really do not expect your approval. I'd just like you to listen. Recently, I have been able to identify a need and I've learned to fulfill it. I feel good about myself. Listen to what happened."

When telling the story, notice the feelings that are aroused as you say positive loving things about yourself. You may want to keep a journal of these experiences to refer to when things aren't going well.

Chapter 5

SELF, REACHING

✓ *To know courage is to understand fear.*

Just as your opinions and shoe size have changed over the years, so will your self-image. However, changing your self-image is not easy. The old ways are comfortable and familiar, even when they are not working. There are two major reasons why people are reluctant to change: fear of failure and fear of the unknown.

Think of the trapeze artist swinging from one bar and flying to the next. The trapeze artist experiences a moment in time when the unknown and possible failure must be faced.

When trying to change, imagine yourself as the trapeze artist. Visualize your hand on the bar and sense the security of the grasp before you leap. You can do it. An element of risk is part of change. It's not just the obvious fear of failure; it's also the moment in time when you let go of old ways and begin new ones. Once you begin to trust your own perception and judgment, you are on the road to change. It may be risky to change, but it is an even greater risk not to change. Look at the change in Barbara's life.

Barbara, the youngest child of an alcoholic, lost her only available parent when her mother died. At age nine, she began housekeeping for her three brothers and absentee father. Bright and anxious to please, she became a model housekeeper and an excellent family cook.

Layers and layers of good deeds covered the pain from the loss of her mother. Exemplary behavior solicited many rewards and approving responses.

As Barbara grew, her self-image and self-esteem were defined by the creative and competent ways she cared for others. Approval from other people was linked to her own self-approval; her self-esteem was dependent on and vulnerable to the whims of others.

In addition, Barbara had created an idealized and perfectionistic standard of expectations for herself. While Barbara was feeling responsible for the well-being of others, she was unaware of her own feelings.

Upon high school graduation, she married and continued her life patterns with her husband and a new set of children—her own. Her behavior patterns of being an exemplary wife and mother continued throughout her 25 years of marriage. The crossroads came when her adult children left home to start their own lives. Barbara was one step beyond the empty-nest syndrome; she was in the midst of an identity crisis. No one needed her in the ways she defined herself. She didn't have another plan. Her children were gone and her marriage had a big hole in the middle. Her life appeared to have little or no purpose.

After consulting a therapist and a lawyer, Barbara decided divorce was not the answer because she really loved her husband despite the staleness of the marriage. The only place left to look for the answer was within herself. She knew there was something inside her that would help in the next step of her journey. She made a commitment to therapy to find an answer.

As the sessions unfolded, Barbara discovered a corner in herself where she kept a collection of unexpressed feelings. When her mother died, she became the best little girl. She thought, "If I take care of everyone, then maybe they won't leave me like Mommy did." Of course a little girl could imagine that kind of abandonment and try to do everything in her power to prevent such a trauma.

Barbara's story demonstrates the way an adult can possess a version of that same fear. Barbara's fear of abandonment motivated her to take care of everyone so she would not be left alone. But her children did leave, and her worst fear was realized.

Barbara had never been alone before. Much to her surprise, she discovered she had all the talents and resources necessary for her own personal growth and development. But could she be there for herself in the way she had learned to be there for others? And could she take care of herself without feeling she was selfish and irresponsible?

In order for Barbara's change to be successful, she needed to learn the following:

To accept she had a hidden trauma from her childhood that impacted her adulthood.

To trust her own feelings and judgments.

To give self-approval without feeling guilty.

To feel her worth does not depend on doing things for other people.

To spend time alone and enjoy her own company.

To renew her relationship with her husband.

To free herself from the boundaries and limits of her past.

And to understand that though it is risky to find new ways to relate to herself and her family, it is even riskier never to change.

Chapter 6

SELF, ALONE

✓ *Alone, you are free to be your true self.*

People are afraid to be alone for different reasons. While Barbara was afraid to be alone because she had childhood fears of abandonment, Kathy didn't like to be alone because she didn't feel comfortable with herself.

For some, being alone is an acquired skill, requiring personal strength and commitment.

Remember, life does not provide a constant companion. At one time or another, all people will find themselves alone. By preparing for this moment, rather than waiting for it to come up unexpectedly, you may find that being alone isn't so bad after all.

Practice. Next time you prepare dinner for yourself, set the table using your fine china, your favorite candlesticks, and a cloth napkin. When guests come to dinner you set the table for them. Do it for you.

Or go to the movies alone. That's one of the toughest alone activities because it means being alone in a large group. People feel lonely in large groups because they devalue being alone. Say to yourself, "I did not bring a friend to the movies, I brought me! That's just as good."

If you make being alone a positive experience, any associated discomfort and fear will disappear.

One of our favorite books on the subject is *Solitude, A Return To The Self,* by Anthony Storr. In it, Storr describes creative pursuits in the arts, the sciences and in nature that shape personal satisfaction, regardless of personal relationships.

In addition to developing the creative process during moments of solitude, Storr also discusses "the authentic and true self." In many social and professional situations, you may need to present a false self, because it isn't always appropriate to express the way you really feel. Sometimes you can be so busy responding to others that you don't respond to yourself. When you are alone, there is no pretending necessary; you can be in touch with your true self.

Chapter 7

SELF IN TRANSITION

✓ *Although others trust you to care for them, you can be trusted to care for yourself too.*

Your behavior is also important to your self-esteem. Low self-esteem often results in a high level of dependent behavior. Therefore, higher levels of independent thought and activity trigger higher levels of self-esteem and lower levels of dependent behavior.

Dependency means more than the obvious drug and alcohol addictions. Many people are dependent upon food, work, friends, lovers, sex. Any thought or ritual that creates a pattern of obsessive-compulsive behavior maintains a negative and low self-esteem.

Sarah, an only child of hard-working parents, thrived on receiving an immediate reaction to every-thing she did. She craved acknowledgment, approval and appreciation for her accomplishments. This start-ed when Sarah was only a toddler, and she learned to read people through facial expressions, tone of voice, body language and eye contact. She became masterful at "people reading." But she never learned to read herself, instead seeing herself only through the eyes of others.

Sarah developed a progressive dependency on signals from her parents, teachers and friends. This dependency interfered with the usual steps for growth: looking at choices, sorting out preferences and then selecting what fits. Sarah never experienced this process. Not only was she distrustful of her judgment, but frequently she was unsure of her choices.

Problems arose when Sarah, now a young adult, tried to establish a relationship with a man. She needed his approval and attention in order to feel good about herself in the relationship. Sarah was relentless in her efforts to please—preparing special dates, cooking gourmet dishes, dressing to his likes and responding to and accepting his moods like a good little girl. Hurt and puzzled to see his attentions wane and cool as her drive to please reached a peak, Sarah asked, "Can anyone ever love me enough?" An inner voice whispered in response, "How can anyone love me if I don't love myself?"

Sarah needs to discover that two whole persons are needed to successfully participate in one healthy relationship.

Chapter 8

SELF IN RELATION-SHIPS

✓ *When you give up your thoughts and feelings for another person, you give up all you really have—yourself.*

The dynamics of an intimate relationship greatly impact the maintenance of high self-esteem. A healthy relationship enhances and encourages positive self-esteem. Both partners are responsible for their own self-esteem and are sensitive to each other's esteem issues.

Evaluate your self-esteem within your intimate relationship by completing the following worksheet:

	Yes	No	At Times	Not Sure
I feel I am loved for who I am and not for what I do within my relationship.	◯	◯	◯	◯
My thoughts and feelings are accepted, respected and considered.	◯	◯	◯	◯

	Yes	No	At Times	Not Sure
My sense of privacy is accepted in both mental and physical spaces.	○	○	○	○
I feel free to disagree with my loved one without penalty.	○	○	○	○
When I make mistakes, we discuss my behavior, not my character traits.	○	○	○	○
Our responsibilities in our relationship are based on our strengths and weaknesses, not gender.	○	○	○	○
We value and plan for alone time within our relationship without guilt.	○	○	○	○
We try to be true to our natures and act in the best interests of our relationship.	○	○	○	○

	Yes	No	At Times	Not Sure
I don't feel the same about myself when my loved one is not with me.	◯	◯	◯	◯
My love relationship validates me in the eyes of others.	◯	◯	◯	◯
My love relationship validates me in my own eyes.	◯	◯	◯	◯
I do not feel I have to prove my worth to my loved one.	◯	◯	◯	◯
I feel devastated when my loved one rejects me sexually.	◯	◯	◯	◯
I feel hurt when my loved one rejects me sexually.	◯	◯	◯	◯
I feel my loved one has a problem when I've been rejected sexually and then try to understand where my loved one is coming from.	◯	◯	◯	◯

	Yes	No	At Times	Not Sure
My loved one is resistant to change. I feel reluctant and hesitant to explore changes for myself.	◯	◯	◯	◯
I need some degree of caretaking to be assured of the love in our relationship.	◯	◯	◯	◯
My loved one encourages me to enhance my self-esteem at home and in the workplace.	◯	◯	◯	◯
My opinion is of value in our discussions regarding our relationship's direction.	◯	◯	◯	◯
I feel free to say no to my loved one without penalty.	◯	◯	◯	◯
When I do something benefitting only me, my partner is not resentful.	◯	◯	◯	◯

	Yes	No	At Times	Not Sure
When my loved one has a wonderful experience exclusive of me, I feel jealous.	○	○	○	○
I do not feel on trial in this relationship.	○	○	○	○
I appreciate criticism from my loved one that is in my best interest.	○	○	○	○
I do not participate in verbally or physically hurtful behavior.	○	○	○	○
I respect the relationships my loved one values exclusive of ours: family, friends and colleagues.	○	○	○	○
My view of myself is equal in value to the view held by my partner.	○	○	○	○

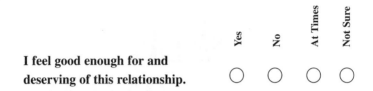

	Yes	No	At Times	Not Sure
I feel good enough for and deserving of this relationship.	○	○	○	○

Look back over the way you responded to the preceding statements. Though there is no "answers guide" to tell you the ideal number of "yes," "no" or other responses, you should consider your feelings about each of your answers. Are you satisfied?

Bring your positive and valuable self to your relationships. If you are the only one working toward change, remember that others may be critical of you. They don't have a need for you to change. It's your need to change.

Some relationships can compromise self-esteem. Giving to your partner has to be in balance with giving to yourself. The danger is giving up too much of yourself for the relationship.

When you know you are doing the best you can, then you must promise yourself not to be intimidated by anyone at any time. Others may try to judge you, control you or tell you what to do. Don't accept it. As Eleanor Roosevelt said in 1937, "No one can make you feel inferior without your consent."

Chapter 9

SELF, HARMED

✓ *When you are hurt by others, you lose your power. Take back your power through discipline and self-control.*

When a child is a victim of emotional or physical abuse, the pain may cast a shadow on the steps leading to adulthood. For many childhood victims, letting go of the pain is not always possible for three reasons:

1. The pain is incorporated into the self-image and personality patterns.

2. The victim has created a punishment/reward system (i.e., I have been hurt so much I deserve more hurt/ice cream/a drink/a gift/sleep).

3. Keeping the memory alive bonds the victim to the past.

Letting go of the pain is not easy, nor is the direction clear. In order to go forward, you have to go backward. This means first reliving the pain and expressing the anger, then mourning the losses.

Completing this task can be overwhelming. Starting anew, lighter but without a familiar frame of reference, is risky. However, keeping the pain keeps you a victim long after the trauma has ended. One yoga teacher commented that children are victims and adults are volunteers.

Harry was the second child of two alcoholic parents. Although he had an older brother, 15 years was too wide a gap to develop a relationship. He saw himself as an only child.

When his father came home, the six-pack came out of the refrigerator. Some nights his parents invited Harry to join them, giving him a small glass of beer. On the nights Dad drank too much he went to bed early, leaving Mom and Harry in front of the television set.

At first, his mother began to lie down beside Harry before he went to sleep. As a second-grader, he didn't mind that too much. As the years progressed, however, she began to fondle him, kiss him and sexually arouse him. He returned her affection. These episodes didn't happen regularly or often, but they did occur. Harry most remembers the pleasurable sensations, which were quite intense for a young boy. When he was 15, he refused to lie down with his mother anymore. Inside, he felt these incidents were weird and unnatural.

That year, Harry began to date and search for a missing feeling. He yearned for that intense and plea-

surable feeling. When he found a girlfriend, they stayed together until they married after high school graduation. Within a year, these two teenagers had a child. As the pleasurable feelings grew less intense and less frequent, the relationship waned and faded.

Harry left his wife in search of the "feeling." Harry, now age 50, with three marriages and many short- and long-term relationships behind him, finally stopped to observe himself and ask, "What is it that I want from a woman? How can I keep that feeling going so I don't have to keep moving on?" This feeling, which began in his early childhood and grew more intense through adolescence, stemmed from the intimate contacts with his mother. The feeling was expressed outside of an appropriate relationship. The feeling was a singular sensation, often bigger than his years or his capacity to handle it. At 50, Harry is stuck with a 15-year-old's unexamined and undefined emotions, intermingled with a sense of shame.

Emotionally, sexually and psychologically, Harry remains 15, frozen in time at the age when sexual inter-action with his mother stopped. Because this desirable feeling is unhealthy, Harry finds himself torn between wanting it and wanting to be healthy. Although he is still looking for this sensation in current relationships, intellectually Harry knows it cannot be attained.

There are many other ways in which a parent-child relationship can be out of balance. Sometimes mother-daughter bonds do not adhere to meet the demands of time and personalities. When there is a gap in the relationship, there seems to be a universal need—almost a quest—to feel united in a mother-daughter connection. Rachel's story tells of a quest for this connection.

Rachel was born at the end of June, following her mother Iris's high school graduation. Unable to care for her baby, Iris gave Rachel to Emily, Iris's older sister and a strict disciplinarian. Throughout her childhood, Rachel lived in two separate worlds: her aunt's rigid and conservative household alternated with fun visits from her young mother. As Rachel matured, she often accompanied Iris to bars and clubs. Rachel's father had long since left her mother, and Iris's many boyfriends provided the only male contact Rachel ever knew because her surrogate mother was asocial.

At age 11, during one of their nights out, Iris left with a man after finding Rachel a ride home. Instead of taking her directly home as he had promised, the man took Rachel to a vacant lot, violated her and left her there. Rachel hid in the bushes until morning and then found her way home. Shortly after this trauma, Iris left town with her new boyfriend. Rachel was devastated. The pain of maternal abandonment was only eclipsed by the pain of sexual violation.

As any child would, Rachel felt responsible for both incidents. "If only" thoughts slipped in and out of her mind as she tried to focus on her school life. Since Iris left no forwarding address, Rachel lived a fantasy that her mother's next visiting day would be soon. The only constant in her life remained Aunt Emily, who further restricted Rachel's activities as she went on to high school.

Rachel's perceptions about herself and her life experiences were distorted. In order to be loved, she thought she had to be what other people wanted her to be. If she didn't do something right or even good enough, the other people in her life would go away.

While Rachel's experience is way outside the limits of the norm, her thought pattern is well within the range of the norm. Young people are usually encouraged to meet the demands of parents, neighbors, teachers and relatives. In order to be accepted and gain the approval of important adults, children discover what the members of each circle want for membership.

Here it is clear that self-image and self-esteem can be defined by meeting the demands and pleasures of others. The only measure of goodness a child perceives during the formative years is an approving adult's smile. At some critical point in those formative years, the approving smile must be internalized by the child and seen as self-approval. When this connection does not take place, the search for approval from other adults, especially those in authority positions, remains fixed.

In the case of Rachel, her pre-teen trauma damaged her thinking patterns and emotional pathways. As a young adult, she was reunited with her mother and her quest for bonding was reopened. But that bond was an unattainable goal. Iris was always a visiting mother; she could never stay.

"If I give up my mother, I have no one," cries Rachel, frozen at age 11, the impacted time of trauma.

Chapter 10

SELF, COPING

✓ *When faced with a problem, break it down into parts. Deciding what part of the problem belongs to you is the key to coping effectively.*

Throughout years of research on the dynamics of high and low levels of self-esteem, we conducted workshops to help participants identify the typical areas in which they feel most vulnerable. The following discussions include responses to the statement: Describe the situation in which you feel your self-esteem is vulnerable.

Trying To Please

"My self-esteem gets knocked down when I give 150% and it's not good enough for my family. Then I get mad at myself because I don't look out for number one—me."

Trying to please other people can be very discouraging. It's important for you to place yourself on the list of people you are trying to please. At the very least, give yourself a turn.

Authority

"My self-esteem is most vulnerable when a person in authority shouts at me."

When you were young, people in authority had power over you. Now this can't happen unless you agree to it. A boss can tell you what to do, but no one has power over you unless you let go of your own power.

Alcohol

"I feel vulnerable when my husband is in a bad mood and drinks too much."

It is difficult to control the behavior of other people, especially when drinking is involved, because the alcohol takes control. Try to accept that you are only responsible for your own behavior.

Communication

"My personal power feels at risk when I hold back from telling my children or grandchildren something because I don't want to lose the relationship."

It can be painful to hold feelings inside and not express yourself. At times, relationships are enhanced when people give themselves permission for personal expression. If they do get angry at what you say, that's okay. You can agree to disagree. But you will probably not lose the relationship.

Confrontation

"I lose my self-esteem when I'm involved in a confrontation or when I avoid a confrontation altogether."

Confronting someone is difficult because it means you have to deal with your anger. However, holding anger can be hurtful to yourself. It is often better to confront someone and get it over with than prolong the anxiety with worry or avoidance.

Perception

"My self-esteem is most vulnerable when someone close to me accuses me of a certain behavior that I feel is not true. The statement is based on the person's perception and I feel powerless to change it."

It can be frustrating to have people think untrue thoughts about you. You can try to discover why the person has that perception, and you can offer more information of your own as to why you feel that perception is wrong. Unfortunately, however, you cannot always change what another person believes.

Praise

"I feel insecure about the value of what I do, say or write unless someone acknowledges or praises me, and, therefore, I remain afraid to act."

Feeling insecure and feeling afraid are two feelings that feed off each other. The more you feel the first, the stronger the other becomes. Looking for approval from others keeps these two feelings in place. Try looking within yourself for approval.

Alone

"My self-esteem is okay, but I feel very bad when I'm in a crowd alone."

If you look at your statement and eliminate the word "crowd," you have a closer view of when you feel lonely. If you are comfortable with yourself to start, you will feel comfortable alone or in a crowd.

Saying No

"My self-esteem is most vulnerable when my family places demands on me and I cannot say 'no.' I am my own worst enemy."

Saying "no" to people you love doesn't feel good. At times, saying "yes" to yourself means saying "no" to someone else. The next time your family needs you, give everyone a turn, and then give yourself a turn.

Chapter 11

SELF AS TIME MANAGER

✓ *Leaving yourself with little or no personal time diminishes your inventory of energy, creativity and power.*

In light of all the things in your life you have no power over, there is one area you can gain control of—your time. Time management is a learned skill, one at which you can become masterful. The secret is in the strategy of time segments.

Make a list of the people who demand your time. Now, at this moment, place yourself at the top of the list.

If you have learned to give away your power, you have probably also learned to give away your time. Overcommitted schedules, compulsive helping and excessive availability are characteristics of everyone's life at some time or another. However, if this sounds like your life all the time, then it's important to acknowledge that this is a problem. Perhaps a new perspective would help you schedule time for yourself on a daily basis.

Daily Schedule

Make An Appiotment With Yourself

7 AM	Prepare for work	
8	Travel to work	*Morning Appointment Time*
9	Work	*Take 10 Minutes For You*
10	Work	
11	Work	*Mid-day Appointment Time*
12	Lunch	*Take 10 Minutes For You*
1 PM	Work	
2	Work	*Afternoon Appointment Time*
3	Work	*Take 10 Minutes For You*
4	Work	
5	Travel home	*Evening Appointment Time*
6	Prepare dinner	*Take 10 Minutes For You*
7	Family time	
8	Family time	
9	Prepare to end the day	*Night time Appointment Time*
10	Prepare for bed	*Take 10 Minutes For You*
11	Bed	

Following this example will give you ten-minute blocks of time totaling one hour each day. The purpose of this time is to re-energize and avoid burn-out by the end of the day. You can stretch your body, meditate, read a magazine, take a walk, listen to music or do any other relaxing activity. You should not answer the telephone, do chores, worry, work or do anything that will interfere with your relaxation.

In order to control your time more effectively, it is important to be aware of the time-stealers in your life. Look at the following list of time-stealers and identify the culprits in your own life.

- telephone
- inertia
- sleep escapes
- negative feelings
- inadequate task delegation
- gossip
- uncomfortable clothing
- television
- denial
- procrastination
- mood-altering substances like coffee, sugar, chocolate or drugs
- perfectionism
- unorganized errands
- insomnia
- physical fatigue from poor lighting, poor nutrition, poor posture

For this week eliminate three time-stealers. Continue cutting each week until your list is as lean as possible.

For tips in using time efficiently, examine the following time-savers.

- prepare for time-stealers
- do more than one thing at a time
- know your peak-times
- live in the present
- make "to-do" lists
- arrange medical appointments to be first or last
- be prompt
- plan your day
- categorize clutter
- differentiate wants from needs
- make realistic schedules

We are all given one day at a time; it is our right and responsibility to determine how it is used.

Remember, "Yesterday is a cancelled check and tomorrow is a promissory note. Only today is cash in hand to spend meaningfully."

Chapter 12

SELF AS CEO

✓ *Your appointment book is the script that determines your life story. Write yourself in it.*

A healthy and balanced self-esteem requires careful planning. Care about and respect yourself enough to change. Use the following worksheet as your individual plan for positive self-esteem.

1. Identify three goals to work toward developing a positive self-esteem.

2. Select a time frame for evaluating these goals (one to three months).

3. Pick a nonjudgmental listener to call for support. Tell your plan to this person. Ask your support person to listen and not to advise.

4. Choose a daily relaxation time (from 30 to 60 minutes).

Rotate among several activities for your private time such as the following:

- Meditate
- Do deep breathing exercises
- Stretch
- Listen to music
- Read
- Write
- Do crossword puzzles
- Work on craft projects
- Do visualization exercises

Gifts For You

- Buy yourself flowers
- Take a bubble bath
- Wear your favorite color frequently
- Keep a favorite photo nearby
- Unplug the phone for one hour
- Cook yourself a special dinner
- Listen to the rain
- Reread a favorite book
- Fly a kite
- Put aside your routine

Make a difference in your life with

Changes
THE RECOVERY LIFESTYLE MAGAZINE

CHANGES is the only national magazine that keeps you informed about the latest and best in personal growth and recovery.

CHANGES offers thought-provoking feature stories and exciting special sections. Plus six enlightening features aimed at helping you heal and strengthen the important aspects of your life: Feelings, Relationships, Body, Working, Self-Esteem and Spirit.

Order *CHANGES* today and get our special offer to you: One year of *CHANGES* (six bi-monthly issues) for just $18.00. That's 40% off the basic price, and a fraction of the annual newsstand price.

Clip and mail this coupon to: *CHANGES* Magazine, P.O. Box 609 Mount Morris, IL 61054-0609
Or simply call 1-800-998-0793 (please refer to code RCHC64).

About The Authors

Maida Berenblatt has been a psychotherapist in private practice on Long Island for the past 15 years. She is a consultant and counselor for workshops in personal growth and development, including stress management and self-esteem.

Alena Joy Berenblatt has a master's degree in journalism and is a journalist in New York City. As Maida's daughter, she listened to anecdotes of personal growth and development sprinkled throughout her growing years.